I GOT YOU

*Restoring Confidence
in Love and Relationships*

Written by

Rob Hill Sr.

Spirit Filled Creations

Copyright Page

Spirit Filled Creations
3509 Kids Court
Chesapeake, Virginia 23323-1262

Copyright © 2013 by Rob Hill Sr.

Cover design by Brandon Jones
Photography by Marque Robinson

For information or to book an event contact publisher via email
SpiritFilledCreations7@gmail.com

Manufactured in the United States

ISBN 978-0-9653696-6-4 (paperback)

*This book is dedicated to **Love**...*

From this day forward

I promise not to let the fears of my mind

force me to backspace the words from my heart...

ever again.

Acknowledgments

This book would not be possible without my incredible family. Your unconditional love, support, and countless sacrifices have been my driving force. Everything I believe about love and happiness comes from you.

To my grandfather, the late Robert Wayne Jewell. You showed me the makings of a real man. Thank you for every single lesson you taught me. I could never repay you for the way you protected and provided for the women I hold so dear to my heart. I am proud of who I am because I know your blood runs through my veins. Your presence alone could move mountains. And though you're no longer physically beside me, I feel you walking with me every day of my life.

To the extraordinary women who have molded me. Darlene Jewell, Daiquiri Jewell, Monique Anderson, Derricka Corbin, Latoria Boone, Elise Hillman, Jewell Boone, Brianna Anderson, Ahmore Anderson, and Desirae Corbin. Because of you, I know the value of a good woman and the power of her love.

To my brothers who were there for me when I had nothing. I'll never forget it! Thank you for always pushing me closer to my destiny.

To the amazing Victoria Davis. You didn't have to invest in my ability to improve as a writer, but you did and I grew because of it. Thank you for believing in me, and this book project.

Lastly, a heartfelt thank you to everyone who has connected with my work and supported me. Every day I strive to get better and I pray you will continue to grow with me on my journey.

Contents

Introduction

In each of us, there is a unique gift—something special for us to leave our mark on the world. Life has a way of making us feel alone. The hard times come and make us feel cold and secluded. But we aren't alone. Regardless of how down we get, how many people betray our trust, or how many times we are told to be patient, we are not alone. When you find that you are trapped in that feeling of loneliness, ask yourself, "Am I lonely because no one cares, or am I lonely because I'm not strong enough to let anyone get close enough to care?" What I found is that we shy away from sharing what we really feel. We avoid showing what we really desire. We don't want to be the one who dropped the ball and left everything we touched to rot. We don't want to be the one who was a constant disappointment, or the reason every heart we connected with got broken. None of us want to be someone else's regret. Instead, we want to give the best of ourselves to show others that they will be valued and appreciated by us. We want to nurture the bonds we build because what we ultimately want is it to experience real love. But in order to have it, we have to redefine what it means to love someone. You and I are more than mere life changers; we are heart healers. We have to believe that better is possible, and encourage each other's growth until we've not only reached our potential, but surpassed all that we've believed to be possible.

This book isn't about playing a game to get what you want. It's about you looking at yourself and finding ways to learn how to grow as an individual. I cannot tell you every single step you should take to get you to where you are trying to go in life. But what I can do is make sure you have enough confidence to trust your own judgments, regardless of past mistakes. I want you to understand that it's okay to be exactly where you are right now, whether you are single or in a relationship. Appreciate where your journey is taking you, but be able to identify areas that need to change. I want you to read this book and have a better understanding of the present. I want you to know that trying to get it right is a constant process. We never arrive at a place of knowing it all. For as long as we are alive, we are challenged to grow, learn, evolve, and mature. Love is a decision, not a destination. It's not something you stumble upon. You must choose to walk in it, give to it, and become it. Each of us travels a different path to find the love we are searching for. Some find what they are looking for instantly, while others must jump over a few hurdles before realizing they have finally found something special. In essence, we are all just working towards what we believe we deserve— our fair chance at love and happiness.

From this moment until forever, I am hoping for more. Not just for me, but for you, and the hearts of our generation. You are still alive and able to read these words for a reason. Whatever happened to you didn't kill you. It may have hurt, but it wasn't strong enough to break you; so don't allow it to stop you from moving forward. You are more than your pain. You are more than your heartbreaks; and you are so much more than your mistakes. Hope is beyond fear. Faith is beyond disappointment. Love is beyond pain. Persistence is beyond rejection. Dedication is beyond doubt. I am making a commitment to do whatever it takes to get it right and help you do the same. I'm not coming to save you from where you are, or promising that everything I say is going to automatically make your life, or your relationship, perfect. But I am willing to share my heart and make everything that I've learned, up until this point, plain so that you and I can walk together on this journey to finding the love our hearts so desperately want and need.

I've wondered, for some time now, what the greatest prize life had to offer could be. I'm not sure if I know, but I am certain that the greatest prize for my life, at this very moment, would be the freedom to love without the presence of fear, the boldness to try without the worries of rejection, and the wholeness to exist without the suffocating presence of loneliness. I hope this inspires you, and if nothing else, gives you the courage to believe that ***I Got You.***

PART I

The
Beginning

We all know that feeling— the sigh of relief when we meet someone who sparks an interest in us. We reminisce on the times we thought we'd found something long-lasting in other relationships and ended up being disappointed. Or the times we cursed the opposite sex, swearing we would never open ourselves up to the possibility of dating again, let alone trust someone to get close to our heart. However, despite our rantings and ravings about being alone for the rest of our lives, as time passes, we realize we are ready to make ourselves available to the opportunity of getting to know someone again. But, not just anyone—someone *new*! Although we are always unsure of what the end result will be, each of us secretly hopes that this person will reveal a truth about us that we desperately want to believe—that we are worthy of both loving and being loved in return.

So, you've met, exchanged contact information, and finally agreed to hang out. After a couple of dates, the thoughts that this could possibly be something real start flooding your mind. Before you know it, you can't stop thinking about the person and wanting to be around them *all the time*. We don't know how liking this new person more and more seems to happen so quickly because the best feelings are often times the hardest to describe. This is what makes the challenge of new beginnings so uncertain. Will the next date be as great as the last one was? Will the ex you thought you were done with call right when you feel you have moved on? Will your new interest leave you hanging the minute they start feeling that you could be too good to be true? Are they so afraid of taking a chance that they cringe at the thought of actually having to finish what they've started with you?

Through our senses, we learn to avoid things that have the ability to hurt us. Through sight, sound, smell, taste, and touch, we spend our entire lives naturally avoiding things that can cause us harm. However, when it comes to the senses of our heart, we find ourselves trying again and again to find love, in spite of what we have previously experienced, good or bad. Love is the drink, and disappointment is the hangover. We say we're never drinking from the cup of love again, but we go back because we're intoxicated with the kind of hope that always believes next time can, and will be better for us. We return to love because no matter how many disappointments we have experienced, we know that there is nothing else that satisfies us the way it does.

Starting over, for most of us, is scary. But, as much work as it requires, new beginnings are new blessings. When we are afforded another chance at love, it is an opportunity to put to use what we have learned from our previous mistakes. So what if it's unfamiliar? Who cares if it forces us to step out of our comfort zone? Wouldn't you rather take a chance at happiness instead of playing it safe and risking being alone and miserable because of fear? We must learn to find the silver lining in every challenge that our new beginnings bring us. There is more to the story of our hearts than memories of hurt, lies, manipulation, and wasted time from our past. We have to constantly refresh our reality because that's the key to improving the way we perceive love. There is no loss in starting over. You only lose when you're too scared to try.

CHAPTER 1

Do I Deserve a
New Beginning?

The moment we start believing the wrong things about ourselves, we create a negative mentality of what we think we deserve. We remember every flaw, mistake, and shortcoming and start beating ourselves up about it. We replay the times someone trusted us and we betrayed them. There is a constant need to dwell on when we didn't keep our word, or when the chance to do the right thing was presented to us, but we chose to do otherwise. Our memories aren't always fair to our hearts. No man or woman is perfect in the relationship, or in their attempt to make it work. You have to learn how to take responsibility for your role without allowing your past to strip away the value of who you are.

We are all deserving of new beginnings. A clean slate with someone new can be both wondrous and eventful. The routine of being lied to, manipulated, and mistreated gets old. Instead of taking the time needed to heal and try again, we usually go from heartbreak to "I give up" mode. This is a fatal mistake. When you shut down and close yourself off to the world, you're settling. When you are no longer open to the idea of being vulnerable with someone, you're missing out on the chance to let your heart be free. When you refuse to connect with new people and remove the mask of pain, you're shortchanging your chance at the possibility of happiness. Why shouldn't you get another chance to get it right? Why haven't you earned the right to a meaningful relationship? Why does *your* heart have to be the one that turns bitter and cold?

> **We are all deserving of new beginnings.**

You can change everything about who you are by making the decision to stop living as the old you, and embrace being the new, better you. When you take the steps toward a new beginning, it is important that you keep your ears open only to people who support your desire to grow. Some may tell you that you'll never change, or constantly remind you of where you've fallen short in the past. Others may think that your ex was the one for you, but you know that the relationship you left was not benefiting for you or the other person. Whatever the case may be, you cannot mix the paths of old and new together. You are either going to go backwards, standstill, or move forward.

Evaluate what your new beginning represents to you, and about you. This will help to define what you are capable of bringing to the relationship. If your current situation is bringing out the worst in you by magnifying the same bad traits you've always exemplified, it's probably not something you should continue to pursue. If you find that you're really not ready to date yet, don't. But if you see that your fears and concerns are changing and you are willing to at least *try* to love again, take that chance. It's okay to admit that starting over is hard. You have to find someone worth investing your time into, learn their habits, tendencies, likes and dislikes. It's not an overnight process and it shouldn't have to be in order for you to trust it. What's more important to you— starting over in hopes of building something great or wasting time going in the same circles over and over again? The truth is, we would all rather be with someone than be alone. Don't compromise or give up on the desires of your heart. You deserve to be happy!

CHAPTER 2

How Do I Know This Time Will Be Different?

The truth is, you don't know for certain that this time will be different because you're the only person you have control over in a relationship. Although previous situations hurt you and left you disappointed, it's in the past. You can't change it. Now, you probably did some things you promised you would never do, and said some things you wish you could take back. It's possible you even held back from saying some stuff you wish you had gotten off your chest. But, your approach to how you will handle the next person should not be an unrealistic list of all the things you expect to be different. Don't

11

make the mistake of thinking you know it all based on what you've gone through. The difference is not always in what the other person should or shouldn't be doing. It begins with you. *How do I love differently this time? How do I connect in a more intimate way? How do I build a better foundation for the next relationship?* These are all questions you must ask yourself.

Things will only turn out as differently as you allow them to. Who are you going to be for your heart— the one who heals it, or the one who hurts it? The difference between who you are and who you're willing to become will be the largest determining factor in whether this time, or the next time, will be different than the last time. Your journey in life is nothing more than a trail of lessons you learn along the way that shape who you are as an individual. Some of those lessons will bring out the best in you, and some of them will show you areas where you need to grow and mature.

> *Who are you going to be for your heart?*

Your past is not there to haunt you or destroy you. Think of it as a mirror. Look at yourself and see how you can get better. What are the things you like about yourself? What are your areas of improvement? When you think about it, it's really not about the next relationship being different. It's more about what you're willing to do to create a better opportunity for yourself. What good is it to wonder if things will work out another way if you haven't put forth the necessary effort to change? What good is looking for something different if you're just going to handle everything the same way you did before? Asking for change is an exercise in futility—you must become it.

The most you can hope for is a relationship that inspires growth and challenges you to become a better person, partner, and lover. A relationship that increases the passion in you to experience true love will make you *want* to give it your all. Happiness isn't really happiness if it only benefits you. It should allow you to be a blessing to everything else around you. The key to securing a different result is to redefine what it is you know you are capable of giving. Remember, you only control yourself. You can't look for a situation that brings you peace if all you operate with is pride. You can't ask for loyalty, trust, and unconditional love if *your* heart is the only one you're trying to protect. You have to open up and stretch beyond fear, doubt, and uncertainty. Do you really want to know how you can almost guarantee that things will turn out differently the next go round? Be different!

CHAPTER 3

Resist the Urge to Control and Manipulate Things

We only feel the need to try to control the things that we don't trust. The downfall to trying to control everything is, it hinders your ability to enjoy anything. You start playing with every variable to ensure a certain outcome. So, instead of having a relationship, you end up with an emotional science project. It does nothing but frustrate you in the end because you haven't learned anything, challenged yourself in any way, or gotten anywhere as a result of your efforts. All you've done is set yourself up for disaster. You cannot insist on having everything *your* way. *Who are you going to be for*

15

your heart? Who are you going to be for your heart? When your only focus is being in control, your partner will feel the effects of it. Love should not be controlled or manipulated. It is supposed to be enjoyed, given, and shared. It's not love if you want to control it, because that control will eventually feel like a burden. Once the weight of that burden becomes a constant exchange of arguments, disagreements, and finger pointing, a breakup is on the horizon.

> *You're stronger and wiser than you give yourself credit for.*

You have to challenge yourself to take a different approach than the one you usually do. You may be thinking, "but my approach is good ... it works for me." If that is the case, why are you in your current situation filtering through countless relationships trying to secure one that will actually work? You have to trust every experience that has brought you to this point. You have to be willing to make sound decisions from this point forward. You aren't the same naïve person who usually falls for lies. You aren't the same passive person who always gets walked over. You've learned to embrace being alone as a chance to get to know yourself better, instead of an opportunity to wallow in loneliness. You have determined what you deserve, and refuse to accept anything less than that. These are important reminders you have to tell yourself, and you have to be audacious enough to believe what you say. You didn't go through all that you went through for nothing. It was to prepare and propel you forward. You're stronger and wiser than you give yourself credit for. Trust in who you know you are. You don't have to try to change yourself into somebody you aren't just to attract potential partners. We have an odd way of wanting to be loved so badly that we end up manipulating our way into someone's life. It's such a backwards way of thinking. If someone likes you enough to get to know you based on who they perceive you to be, let them. If it doesn't work out, accept it. Don't let the fear of them seeing the real you, and not being able to handle it, be the reason they can't get close to you.

Your focus shouldn't be the thought of things not working out. You should be more afraid of trying so hard to control a situation that you run a good person away. When you manipulate a situation, it's because you're not secure in allowing yourself to be good enough. You're scared that if they get too close, they'll hurt you. When we're afraid of the other person not being good to us, it's often because we know we haven't been the best to ourselves. Fear blocks the beauty of love and all its possibilities. What if they got close and helped you heal! What if they embraced your flaws and made you feel beautiful just the way you are! Fear doesn't protect you, it imprisons you and leaves you all by yourself. All the while, the life you could, and should, be enjoying is passing you by.

> *Trying to control someone will not serve you in any way.*

The best thing you can do is believe that things will work out the way they're supposed to. Everybody is not out to hurt you, or take from you, and play games with your heart. But you won't be able to see this if you're stuck trying to manipulate everybody that comes your way in an attempt to play it safe. We all risk being hurt when it comes to building a relationship with someone. The commonality of heartbreak should be what brings two people closer together. When you know how it feels to be hurt, the last thing you want to do is perpetuate that pain to someone else. Trying to control someone will not serve you in any way. They will never be able to actually satisfy you if you are trying to change them into who you want them to be, instead of allowing them to be who they really are. Love is all about the possibilities of what *can be*. When you try to control and manipulate your relationship, the limitations you set don't allow you, or the other person, to freely experience the opportunities love has to offer.

CHAPTER 4

Fair Chances

Most of us know what it's like to be disappointed by someone we took a chance on. It's a part of life. It's nearly impossible to meet every standard on someone's checklist and still be yourself completely. When you are concerned that the other person will fall short, you hinder their potential to be a valuable addition to your life. The same way you want to be respected for what you bring to the table, others do as well. Far too often, we're scared somebody's not going to like the choices we make, understand our point of view, or agree with everything we say and do. Instead of getting to know them, and balancing out the differences, we quickly decide that they can't be right for us. When you reject someone because they are different than you,

you build a wall with no doors. This forces them to either climb the ever-changing heights of that wall to get to you, or give up and find someone else. Take the time to get to know the person. You can't have a real relationship with anyone unless you're willing to give them a fair chance.

> *Take the time to get to know the person.*

Attempting to have a healthy relationship can only be done when you apply what it takes to build a solid foundation instead of focusing on all the negative things that usually contribute to destroying one. When our own fears influence us to create barriers around someone, we are telling them that they aren't allowed to be themselves. The person you meet and fall in love with will change many times during the relationship. As we mature, our perspectives and opinions about different things will shift. Sadly, most of us have conditioned change to "you're not the person I met," or "you've always done it this way, why do you want to do something new now"? We automatically think of change as a bad thing, but it's not. Embrace your partner's growth as an opportunity to learn new things about them, and they should be open to doing the same with you.

Differences are not the only thing that can hinder us from giving someone a chance. Similarities to someone from our past can also be an issue that we have a hard time dealing with. We've all had different experiences that have tailored our views on what we believe it takes to obtain a healthy relationship. The first "real" relationship we have is usually the most selfless one because we become so engulfed in wanting to love our significant other that we are willing to overlook all the negative things about them— even if what we see are clear red flags. Our entire life revolves around being with them and making them happy. When that relationship turns out to be a huge letdown, everything we thought we knew about love changes almost immediately. From that moment on, we instantly compare everyone we meet to our ex. While it is wise to identify warning signs early on, it is not safe to paint two people with the same brush solely because they may have similarities. If she has the same color eyes and hairstyle as your ex-girlfriend, that does not mean she will be just like her. If he drives the exact same car and has the same mannerisms as your ex-boyfriend, they are still two different people. The key to avoiding heartbreak again is not being so moved by fear that you run at the sight of minor similarities. If they're not the one for you, let it be for reasons that really matter.

> *Don't get caught up in trying to figure them out too fast.*

So how do you ensure that you are giving someone a fair chance? You give it time, otherwise known as the "getting to know you" stage. Don't get caught up in trying to figure them out too fast. In the same token, don't be so quick to make assumptions based on who you *think* they are. You're not going to know someone in a day, a week, or a month. The foundation of any long-lasting relationship comes from first building a solid friendship, and that takes time. Don't be so eager to make them like everybody from your past. Take them for who they show you they are. Avoid trying to make them your dream come true or fairytale too soon. With time, you may find that the person who started off as your friend is now a confidant, motivator, support system, and someone you can actually seeing yourself growing with. When you allow them an open forum to show you who they are, it also affords you the same respect to be yourself. While every stage of the relationship may not be dreamy, at least you'll know you have something worth pursuing.

PART II

The
Work

Dating really doesn't have to be hard. Sadly, we have a way of unnecessarily complicating things. We make comments like, "I'm not trippin' over it … I like being single." But the truth is, no one wants to be alone. In our hearts, we desire romance because we all long for that connection and the opportunity to be with somebody. It's nice to have someone you can share the ups and downs of life with. There is no such thing as perfect timing, and you'll miss out on something amazing waiting for it. You'll never have all the answers, make enough money, or know enough to be "ready" for love. However, it is possible to find someone you can grow and savor special moments with. The more you convince yourself that you don't need love, the less authentic your love will actually be when you finally have a chance at it. People can't connect with parts of you that you aren't willing to show. Opening up won't kill you. Don't ruin a potentially good thing because you think you have to prove that you don't need anyone. Show some effort and act like you really *want* to be happy. Once you acknowledge that you are ready to not only give love, but receive it as well, that is a good sign that you're equipped to do the work it takes to have a relationship that will last.

A chance is a terrible thing to waste. When you agree to start a relationship with someone, you are initially saying, "I'm ready to put in the work required for both of us to be happy together." Finding someone who will take the time to sincerely get to know you, genuinely care for you, and value you is very rare. We complain about the same things day to day and nothing changes because we're stuck playing the same old games. We acknowledge when we're lied to, and then hide from the truth the minute it challenges us. We complain about consistency, but we don't give anyone a fair chance to prove themselves to us. We look for loyalty, but we aren't willing to open up and show someone that we are worth being loyal to. Believe that you have a right to love and happiness, and then start taking the necessary steps mentally and emotionally to acquire both.

What's important to you? Do you care about building something real, or are you planning to be single forever? Do you believe that you have what it takes to make a relationship work? Or have you been fooled into thinking that you're just supposed to give up and not care? You can't have an "it is what it is," attitude about everything. It's so easy to get caught up in the rat race— date here, flirt there, one night stand, etc.—but when the substance of true love is missing, you're never really getting anywhere. When all the games have been played, are you going to have something to show for it? Will you have had anything worth remembering? Can you be an asset to somebody's life? Can your presence make them better, or happier? If you feel every relationship you have is disposable, that speaks volumes about the value of your time. If you ever plan to have anything worth treasuring, you're going to have to put in the work required to keep it. If you aren't willing to work for love, you don't deserve to have it.

CHAPTER 5

Letting Go of Pride

Pride isn't always a bad thing. When you take pride in how you speak, dress, and things of that nature, you show that care about the way you present yourself. When you take pride in the way you treat people, be it your mannerisms or certain courtesies you offer, that speaks volumes to your character. Taking pride in being attentive, thoughtful, and considerate are positive attributes that we should all have. It's when you mix that type of pride with ego that things can get ugly and you can end up quickly pushing somebody away.

Two of the most damaging areas of pride are asking for forgiveness, and granting forgiveness. An unwillingness to apologize when you know you're wrong is the ultimate sign of selfishness. Not only is this childish and immature, but it's extremely disrespectful and unfair to your partner. If you're too good to apologize then the only person you really care about is you. Likewise, an unwillingness to forgive your partner when they apologize to you is just as bad. The best love is reserved for forgivers. When your partner tries to fix what they have done wrong, be open to forgiving them. You have to be willing to accept that in a relationship, both of you will make mistakes, upset each other, and do many things wrong even when it's not always intentional. Each one of us is flawed and can be expected to mess up. However, you have to love your partner enough to forgive them.

> *... have enough faith to believe they won't walk out on what you've built.*

Another area of pride that can hurt a relationship is being cold and closed off to your partner. Opening up and getting out of your own way doesn't mean you have to reveal every single secret in the first conversation. But it does mean that you have to possess a strong willingness to expose intimate pieces of yourself over time. You may risk being misunderstood, but you have to trust that your partner will be able to accept what you tell them without judging you. In fact, when it comes to love, your ability to open up should cause them to connect with you on a deeper level regardless of what you share. Neither you nor your partner should avail a listening ear to the other, while never being willing to share your own story. You should be comfortable and confident in knowing that they'll still care for you. Communicate those fears and uncertainties, and have enough faith in them to believe that they won't walk out on what you've built.

There's a certain beauty to letting your guard down and being transparent in your relationship. Allow yourself to connect with no boundaries. A willingness to be vulnerable with someone takes courage, but it's worth it. You learn that you don't ever have to hide who you are with them. More importantly, you never have to imprison your heart just to guard it. You can't be who you are and who you want to become at the same time. If the old ways were really working for you, you would have never decided to change them. Your relationship should mean more to you than your pride does. Once you open up, you create a platform for someone to be comfortable opening up to you as well. So instead of being the person who pushes them away, you now become the person they don't want to ever let get away.

CHAPTER 6

How Bad Do You Want It?

You know you're ready for a relationship when you want one for what you can give and not just for what you can get. When you're full of love, you can't help but want an opportunity to share it with somebody else. It's not about wanting a relationship so you don't have to watch movies alone, or so you have somebody to cuddle with during thunderstorms. It's certainly not about wanting someone around just to occupy time and space. After you've worked on yourself enough and you're now willing to work *with* someone else, you're ready. A relationship isn't for the selfish, the weak-hearted, or those who are easily deterred. True lovers don't give up until they find exactly what they're looking for.

> *When you're full of love, you can't help but want an opportunity to share it with somebody else...*

When you say you want a relationship for what you can give, it essentially means you're prepared to be vulnerable. You're not worried about who gets credit for what, or so busy keeping record of who calls the other first, that you create childish competition with your partner. You're focused on the important factors that promote growth spiritually, emotionally, and even professionally. You view their goals and dreams as being just as important as your own. You see their weaknesses as areas you're responsible for helping to strengthen. Their fears are opportunities for you to step up and remind them that they are not alone because they have you. You give your time and attention to that person because you know they're worth the investment. You know that a better them will contribute to a better relationship, so you always support and encourage them in everything they do. If you're all *for* them, you'll have all *of* them. But if you're all for you, then all you'll have is you. *Selfish*ness only guarantees a life of misery and loneliness. *Selfless*ness opens the door to endless possibilities.

If you don't feel like you have anything to give or contribute to another person's life then you're better off single. Two half empty, or half full cups cannot make the other full—where one tries to fill the other, it will be emptying itself. You need to be a full individual and your partner should be full as well. That way, when it's time to pour into each other, both cups will be overflowing. That's the essence of being equally yoked. Both parties must commit to giving, communicating, connecting, and moving forward in ways that build a foundation that will last. That's the only way to have a relationship worth keeping. Don't ask "What have you done for me lately?" but instead, "What have we done for us lately?"

You have to be ready to give. You have to be willing to commit to doing whatever is required to ensure you're putting out everything you expect to receive in return. It can't be for convenience or comfort. The way you give of yourself will inspire your partner to care for you in ways you would have never imagined. The question is, *how bad do you want it?*

CHAPTER 7

It Takes Two

In order for a relationship to work out, two people have to be fully invested in the process. If you're the only one putting in work, the relationship is not going to go far. The key is finding someone who is just as committed as you are to the work, and who understands the value of love the same way you do. Whether it's talking about problems, being adventurous together, or challenging each other to grow in other areas, you need someone who's going to be a willing participant in it all. You shouldn't have to try to change them, manipulate them, or coerce them to invest in strengthening the bond they have with you. If they aren't willing to meet you

41

halfway, or match your efforts in any way, they're making it clear that it's time to move on. You shouldn't be the only one breaking the silence or offering solutions to mutual problems. Two people only giving half of themselves isn't the recipe for a happy relationship— it's the set up for a dysfunctional one. If you have to walk away from them, letting go does not mean you're quitting or giving up on love. It just means you know that you need to find someone who shares similar values and beliefs of what it takes for the relationship to be successful. A person cannot build a relationship alone. It takes two!

> *... you need someone who's going to be a willing participant in it all.*

You can't force somebody you love to see your value, or the uniqueness of what you contribute to their life. They either get it, or they don't. The problem for most people comes in the acceptance phase. You try to talk it out but they aren't willing to hear you out. You drain yourself attempting to change things but they are rarely satisfied with anything you do. You make efforts to get closer and all they do is push you further away. So now what? You can either accept things the way they are, or conclude that it's time to part ways. One of the worst things you can do is stay stuck on somebody who's made it clear that they've moved on with no intentions of taking you with them. While it may seem easier said than done, it's still necessary. You have to be willing to do what's best for your heart and sometimes that requires making tough decisions.

> **They either get it, or they don't.**

Your love is worth working for. It is a privilege for someone to come into your life and be allowed to get close to your heart. Any person you deem worthy enough to share your space with should value it. Knowing your worth is pointless if you make exceptions every time somebody you like doesn't measure up, you're inadvertently selling yourself short. You know what's right for you and what's best for you. You know what adds the most value to you and you have to be strong enough to stand by that. Stop lowering your standards. If they aren't bringing anything to the table, you have to let them eat alone. If either one of you show up empty handed, that leaves the other one walking away empty hearted. Bring the best of you to the table and be willing to show what you have to offer! The disappointments of the letting them go may hurt, because you saw so much potential in them. It's possible that they even made you happy for a short period of time. But, don't allow yourself to be tricked and toyed with. There is a difference between quitting and an ending. Quitting happens when you stop trying before you've exhausted all possibilities. Ending a relationship is recognizing that it's time to move on *after* you've done all you can do. When it's over, it's over— there's nothing more you can do about it. Require them to do their part, or move on to someone who will be willing to do whatever it takes to be with you.

CHAPTER 8

What Does the Love Inspire You to Do?

When you are in a relationship, you may often wonder what you and your partner are benefitting from being together. One of the easiest ways to measure the value of the relationship is to identify what it inspires you to do. Has it made you want more out of life? Do you want to try new things and grow? Does it make you want to be a better individual and fix bad habits? Has it taught you how to forgive and made you less prideful? Has it increased the value of who you are in any way? A lot of the times we give love a bad reputation for our personal trepidations. We don't want to look at ourselves so we shift the blame every time we fall short, and we lose a lot of special people because of this. If you want to know if a person is any good for you, look at who they inspire you to be and what that inspiration leads you to do. It's all about what they bring out of you. If all you're getting is more anger, confusion, and disappointment, then you need to get out of that situation. Real love does not destroy you. It builds you up! It will increase, inspire, and improve you in every way. This does not mean that it will always be a perfect, or an easy road. But when it's real, things naturally begin to get better and it will be obvious that this person has been a contribution to the new, better you.

> *... love never leaves you disappointed or defeated.*

Love makes you want more out of life. You should desire a love so real that it ignites you first thing in the morning. That type of love makes you feel like everything you *thought* you deserved is no comparison to what you have now been blessed with. True love inspires you to do better; not just for yourself, but for everybody attached or connected to

46

you. Don't get so caught up in trying to "hold it down" for an undeserving person that you sell yourself short of what you could be enjoying with somebody who deserves it. If that works for you, then call it preference, not love. Love makes you feel free, appreciated, valued, and thought of. It is delicately handled, but gripped firmly enough to never let go of.

What you want in your relationship is a bond that inspires you to take chances. If you fail, your partner's encouragement inspires you to have the confidence to keep going and try again. That type of love never leaves you disappointed or defeated. Even when you fall short, you won't question your ability to measure up. That's what real love does! It inspires you to feel unstoppable. And if it doesn't, you don't want it. Love always makes you feel like you deserve the best of what life has to offer. Now is a good time to ask yourself what you and your partner inspire in each other. What is this bond bringing out of you? Who have you become as a result of their love? Your answers should confirm that you love, support, and inspire one another in a way that makes it all worth it.

PART III

The
Illusion

We've all had moments where we've caught ourselves daydreaming about our future with someone. We imagine our wedding and we wonder if it will be big or small, and what we'll wear. Then we'll go on our honeymoon and come back to a new house to that we'll eventually raise our children in. We start to wonder what our kids will look like and how many we'll end up having. And before you know it, we've planned out the next 10 years of our life. But with all these dreams and thoughts there usually comes a certain illusion. You jump from start to finish in your mind so quickly that you find yourself desiring the rewards of love more than you accept the work love requires. You start to think the road to having all of this will be an easy one. And the minute you really believe that, you've set your heart up for some serious disappointment.

Some of us have been so hurt many times that we have become numb to the pain in our hearts. We've trusted people with parts of us that they didn't deserve, given time and energy to people that couldn't appreciate it, and had faith in relationships that crumbled. The relationships we once treasured now seem to fit so perfectly in the box of memories that we try our hardest to conveniently forget. While it may come across that your guard is up and you're playing hard to get, the truth is, you've just learned to be patient and respect the timing of things. You've rushed it and gotten it wrong too many times before, and you're not trying to make that mistake again. But, you have to understand that you're not the only one who's been hurt. You don't need to hide your heart in order to protect it. You just need to be cautious of who you attach your heart to. When it comes to relationships these days, most people over think it. Be careful not to make things more difficult then they need to be. The love you experience will only be as good as the effort you invest in it. The relationships you build will only be as strong as your ability to commit to the work they require. It's all on you!

Realize that there is no such thing as a perfect relationship. Everyday won't be great; every conversation won't be full of laughter; and every moment won't feel like bliss. Don't desire something that's easy. You want something so fulfilling that you never think twice about quitting. You want a love so rewarding that you never consider going on another day of your life without it. You want a relationship so valuable that you confidently ignore your fears and anything else that tries to make you doubt what you have. You can wish for whatever your heart desires. But the moment you understand what it takes to have the love you want, *that* is when it will truly be yours.

CHAPTER 9

Should This Be Easy?

Real love is simple, but it's never perfect or easy. It takes some serious work to merge your life with someone else's. You will have days when you want to walk away. There will be problems, misunderstandings, and all the other things that come with having to put forth effort to maintain something special. But love is a gift. It is magical, beautiful, and so many more incredible things that make it enjoyable and desirable. The good news is, love doesn't have to be hard *all* the time. You should not feel like you are constantly fighting to make the relationship work. If you're giving and it never seems to be enough, you're probably giving to the wrong person. If you holding the relationship together by yourself, what happens if *you* start to fall apart? Who's going to hold you up? Unfortunately, this happens to the best of us. We get intertwined with someone who is no good for us and we wait until we're about to suffocate to finally decide to do something about it. Give up on the hopes of having a relationship that comes with no maintenance, because that's not realistic. However, you can build something that's worth working to keep.

> **The good news is, love doesn't have to be hard all the time.**

Believe it or not, there is someone out there who wants to have a healthy relationship with you. You will meet somebody who will be patient and willing to work with you. Anyone who is focused on adding value to your life will be committed to doing so, without making you regret your decision to be with them. But if all you're getting is more headache and heartache, it's time to re-evaluate the situation. You can't always go with the flow. Having an "it is what it is" mentality won't work if you want to build a strong foundation for a future together. You should never think of it as, "If it works, it works. If it doesn't, oh well." This type of attitude implies that you don't feel you should have to put in work in order for things to work out. But, in the midst of things working out, you also shouldn't be mentally, physically and emotionally exhausted from your relationship. You shouldn't feel empty after every conversation, and you most certainly shouldn't feel used and undervalued every time there's an issue between the two of you.

Love can't show you what you need to see if you choose to keep your eyes closed and pretend that everything is okay. Show your partner you can step up and walk with them on the journey. Assure them that they aren't carrying the weight alone. Be their best friend, accountability partner, and lover. Fight for, not against, one another. Speak life into her when she needs you. Show him you support and believe in him when it matters most. You don't know how to be perfect, so there's no point in trying. But, your partner's importance in your life is shown in the amount of effort you put forth to see them happy. Be compelled to be there for them in the good and bad times. Do things to strengthen the relationship, not things that will leave either of you questioning if what you have together is worth holding on to. When you care about someone, you don't think of it in terms of easy and hard. You do whatever it takes to ensure that they are confident in what they have with you.

CHAPTER 10

Take It or Leave It

What's the first thing we do when we realize we've disappointed someone we care about? We try to make it up to them by giving them something to look forward to. We make promises of what we'll do the next time, and apologize over and over again for what we did to upset them. We leave a trail of hope in their hearts that whatever we did won't happen again. We even know exactly what to say so they won't stay mad at us. But each time we break our promise, we build a case against our ability to be trusted and leave room for our commitment to the relationship to be questioned. Many couples let good relationships die too soon, and they only end up hurting themselves in the process because their next relationship turns out to be nothing but a jumble of unsorted emotions. The love wasn't inspiring or motivating. They felt a sense of responsibility to one another but neither of them had clear direction on where the relationship was going. They stopped growing together and it killed their desire to learn more about one another. Couples who want to stay together commit to each other's growth. They understand that the more their partner grows, the more there is to learn, and love, about them.

What happens is that we become so full of ourselves and confident in our strengths that we create more barriers than bridges for love. You're tough, and you know it all based on what you've experienced, and survived in past relationships. You've seen it all, and you think you can't be affected if someone comes and goes out of your life. Or at least that's what you'd have everyone to believe. While it's great to be sure of yourself, especially after so many have tried to rob you of that security, it's just important to be mindful of the perils that come with being so sure of yourself that you reject the opportunity to grow with someone. The minute you develop the *take it or leave it* mindset, expect to be left far more times that you care to be. When you take that disposition, what you're essentially saying is, "I like you, *but* I'm not changing one thing about myself, or my life, for you." This type of mentality is the theme music to a broken heart.

> *... commit to each other's growth*

People who feel strongly for each other, but feel it's hard to be together, have certain problems because they've allowed negative routines to drain the life out of the relationship. Don't be with somebody that's predictable. Don't be stuck in a situation that never brings any excitement or joy to your life. Love should be electrifying, not boring. Just because the flame is flickering doesn't mean you have to let it burn out. It's not enough just having passionate feelings for one another. Feeling alone

61

can't save a relationship. Get your partner's imagination going. When the relationship loses its excitement, it's time for things to drastically change. Make the effort! Your relationship, no matter how good it is, will never be easy to maintain. It takes a true dedication to your partner. Break the routine of what you normally do. Go out and have fun. Commit to trying something new once a week whether it is cooking dinner, working out, or taking a painting or sculpting class. The goal is to build a stronger bond with each other. While you can easily do any of these things by yourself, include your partner so that you two can continue to grow in your relationship *together*. Genuinely invest in one another and you'll see how being together is much more enjoyable than you ever imagined it could be.

CHAPTER 11

What's In It for Me?

One of the worst mistakes we make when it comes to dating and relationships is thinking that just because we treat someone a certain way, it guarantees that they will automatically reciprocate the same treatment. It's very rare to find somebody who gets it and understands how love works. Unfortunately, the world isn't exactly full of givers. Everyone has their hands open to receive, but very few will extend those same hands to give. When you're always the one giving, there is a tendency for others to get used to it and forget to do more than just take from you. As you get older, you realize that just because you're good to others doesn't mean they'll always be good to you. Some people make themselves easy to cut off. There's no need to get angry at their actions or start thinking of all the ways you can get even. Just thank them for saving you time. If they're unable to hold you down with the same consistency you give them, then you can't keep them around. Anybody like that is no good for you.

> *It's very rare to find*
> *somebody who gets it ...*

Giving with honest intentions does not come with strings or stipulations. You're not keeping track of what's owed to you. You give and you choose to do so without ulterior motives or plans. You do it simply because you're genuine and you take pride in seeing others, particularly your partner, happy. You give because you know what it's like to feel like no one cares. When you give, you show the true depths of what is in your heart. One of the most dominant characteristics of love is selflessness— thinking of others with the same respect that you would want to be thought of. The exact opposite of that is selfishness and nothing positive comes from people who only think about themselves all the time. When the giving starts being taken for granted, and your sincerity is no longer appreciated, don't change who you are by becoming angry and spiteful. Just smarten up and change the taker's role in your life. Because when good people give, they give their best! But when they're done, you won't be able to get another thing out of them.

> *When you give, you show the true depths of what is in your heart.*

When you apply giving and taking to relationships, too many people make the mistake of thinking the good ones will always be there. They selfishly want to believe that when they finally get their act together, start treating people right, and learn to appreciate the little things, you'll be sitting there waiting for them. That's not how it works and it's not how things should be. If you're holding it down for them by always being supportive, encouraging, and dependable, then at the very least, you should be able to expect the same in return. And if they're ungrateful enough to say that you shouldn't have any expectations of them, then they're giving you a clear indication that you don't need them in your life. Why should you be the one who's always paying for everything if he has a job too? Why are you the only one giving gifts and sending small reminders that you're thinking about her? Where is the balance in both people making sure their partner not only hears, "I love you," but feels the love as well. When you wake up in the morning, you should be thinking of ways you can brighten his day. Before your day ends, you should have done something that made her feel like you appreciate the woman she is to you. In a successful relationship, both people are thinking about the other person's needs. As a result, no one is left lacking anything because of each partner has made a commitment to doing whatever is required to make the other feel like they aren't only giving, but getting something in return.

> *There's something about knowing that someone loves you...*

When your partner starts to feel a void in the relationship, because they are lacking something from you, feelings of abandonment and betrayal can easily begin to take root. The crazy thing about being betrayed is, you don't just lose trust in the person. You also start to doubt whether or not you can trust yourself, your judgment, and your emotions. You start resenting that you have a good heart. You start shutting down more and more until even the best parts of you become cold and bitter. Before you know it, you're left trying to figure out who you are. There's nothing wrong with taking a step back to see what's in it for you. What are you getting out of it? Are you being taken for granted or does he balance you out? Is she willing to do her part, or does she expect you do everything on your own? When was the last time your partner did something for you and it wasn't a holiday? Can you remember when they made you feel like you were the best thing to ever happen to them? If you're investing all of you into someone, you should be getting something out of it. Your return should be the corny smile on your face that everyone notices when he calls you at work just to say hello. Or the way you straighten your tie after you've seen a "good morning, babe" text from her on your way out the door. There's something about knowing that someone loves you that makes you feel more confident in who you are. So if you realize you aren't getting anything out of your relationship, it's time to take another look at it and decide if this person is someone you should be with, or someone you'd be better off without.

CHAPTER 12

Then vs. Now

It's amazing how quickly things can change in a relationship. Where do the sparks and infatuation from the beginning go? It's crazy to think that you can go from being excited to talk to a person to feeling like you're forcing the conversation. Before, you couldn't wait to have quality time with each other. Now, date nights have turned into "I'm busy," and the consistent communication has become nothing more than conversations that tend to start, but end up being postponed. Everyone has their own schedule and agenda. One minute you feel like you're floating on cloud nine, and the next minute it seems like all your feelings are being bounced around like a power ball. When you think about where things are in your relationship now, compared to where they were back when you first met, it can be a bit scary to see the changes that have occurred. Couples tend to go from full infatuation to looking for the next best thing. However, there are ways to avoid letting your relationship get away from you.

Maybe we're all guilty of taking things for granted and letting ourselves get too comfortable with what we have. Do we think we can make love appear when it's convenient for us and any other time turn away from it? Maybe we don't realize the effort required to keep a good thing going strong. We often think of happiness as something that finds us instead of it being something we put forth the effort to maintain. After all, happiness is a choice. It's not that the good times fade fast. It's more so that very few can uphold a commitment to making the most of the moments they have with their partner. When you stop investing quality time in your relationship, it's easy to get distracted with so many other things. You'll find yourself giving away time that you used to reserve for your partner. Whether it's spending extra time at work, releasing some steam at the gym, or hanging out with your friends more frequently, you unconsciously stop making them a priority. Before you know it, you don't find each other enjoyable to be around, so the times that you are together feel extremely awkward for both of you.

> **There are ways to avoid letting your relationship get away from you**

When two people are juggling careers, school, and involvement in other activities, you *have* to make time for each other. You can't continue to put it off, and you shouldn't want to. Do whatever it takes to make the necessary sacrifices. If the project at work isn't due until the next week, agree that you will make time on the weekend for her so that she doesn't feel neglected. If you finish the paper for your class and have a couple days of downtime, plan a fun, relaxing activity with him so that he doesn't think he's going unnoticed by you. There's always a way to make it work. True love doesn't have an off switch and it doesn't take breaks. It is respectful and understanding to the other person's individual time and space, but true love is always on, and ready to make itself available. One of the worst things you can do is start taking a good person for granted, especially knowing the effort they deserve to see from you. Don't be the person who misses out on something special now because you are unwilling to make them a priority. It doesn't take much to ensure the person you care about feels exceptional. Be attentive, thoughtful, and consistent in your actions. This not only makes your partner feel appreciated, it shows them you care beyond the usual displays of emotion; you care enough to love them in detail.

PART IV

The
Reality

Love is not about wanting something so badly that you would do anything for it. It's about having the understanding and patience to enjoy what you have without overcrowding it with fears and pressuring it with unnecessary doubts. Love is about being courageous enough to give, strong enough to feel, and secure enough not to hold back from those who deserve the best of you. It is important that you believe something different can happen for you. Forget the games, drop the baggage, and let go of the hurt. Use your time to build genuine relationships instead of looking for excuses to run from good people. Learn how to connect with someone. We don't allow ourselves to be appreciated and valued because we're worried that if we actually experience something real, we wouldn't know what to do with it. Nobody wants to step up and say, "I've made mistakes, but I'm committed to getting better." The reality is, none of us can predict every step of our relationship from start to finish. You have to take it one day, one moment, and one experience at a time.

Be proactive on your quest for love and healthy relationships. Don't give your past all the power. It's time to take your heart back from the bad memories, get your mind off of the irrelevant, and make the changes necessary to be better. You are too beautiful to hide your heart. You're too strong to play it safe and get discouraged just because you've faced a few disappointments. Even if you don't believe it right now, the wait, the pressure, and the hurt, were all for your good. Submit to the process long enough to sacrifice your pride and let God help you along the way. Everything is happening the way it's supposed to. Just stay faithful, ready, and humble because your time is coming. In the meantime, promise yourself that you will not to allow the disappointments to distract you from your destiny or deter you from opening your heart. Above all else, remain true to who you are. Nothing that has happened should take away your ability to love. Don't sit around moping and waiting for somebody to come and improve things in you that you are capable of doing for yourself.

Love is a commitment to protecting someone else's heart with the same passion you use to guard your own. Love will bend and stretch you. It will take you on an emotional rollercoaster at times, but it will never leave you alone. Real love doesn't leave you feeling lonely because it takes no days off. For many, it all comes down to what we know we deserve. If it's understood that you deserve somebody who will make the necessary sacrifices to love you unconditionally, then those who took you for granted were just chances to grow. If you know you deserve happiness and truth, then all the liars were just lessons learned. If you know you're worth the effort, then the ones who fell off are just time saved. It takes going through a few bad situations in order for us to value the chance to treasure a good one. The secret is learning the value of not taking the chances you are given for granted— especially when something good is right in front of you. We have to accept that we won't always make the best decisions when it comes to choosing a partner. Some people are easy to care for but hard to be with. Just don't become jaded in the process. You're not a failure at love. Your experiences will prove that you were being prepared to love, and be loved, better the next time.

CHAPTER 13

Is It Worth It Anymore?

Y ou know when things are different between you and your partner. The little stuff that didn't use to bother you starts to feel like major problems that constantly frustrate you now. The small changes you notice in each other are becoming more and more obvious, while the effort to do better is minimal. When you understand that you cannot make a relationship last, you are able to acknowledge what you will and won't tolerate. You can't force consistency, loyalty, or even honesty. You can't force them to keep their word or to communicate; or even to realize something special is right in front of them. You can't make anyone put up a fight for your heart, or change his or her ways. Take a step back and reflect. If your relationship has turned into a battlefield of mixed emotions, harsh words and constant bickering, you have to ask yourself if it's worth it anymore.

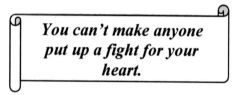

You can't make anyone put up a fight for your heart.

When two people spend a great deal of time together, they become more and more comfortable with being themselves. Three months into the relationship, you were okay with him hanging out late with his friends because you didn't want him to feel like you were trying to spoil his fun. When you met her, you liked the way that she dressed, showing a little skin here and there. Her mystery drew your attention to her. But after couples have been together for a while, they start resenting the things they once admired about each other. Now that you know him better, you see that he's prone to make mistakes. So you want him near you in certain environments because you aren't as confident as you once were in your ability to trust him. Now when she gets dressed up, you ask her who she's trying to impress instead of complimenting her and appreciating the fact that she still cares to look nice for you. And before you know it, you're constantly arguing about the same things over and over again. Why does this happen? Although every couple has their fair share of disagreements here and there, constant disputes and a determination to do what you want to do are sure signs that the relationship is going downhill. Most of the time, we throw the issues under the rug because in our minds, if they are still with us, we don't have to take their needs and wants serious. It's still a form of settling. When you are okay with things being "good enough" in your relationship, you will never have something great. You would think that after all the hurt we have gone through, we would be more successful at being good to one another. Sadly, that's not always the case. Instead, we spend more time looking for easy exits than ways to stay together. The minute they say or do something we don't like, we're sending the text message that it's over.

This vicious cycle is why many of us never get anywhere with love. What happened to hearing each other out? Where does respect and kindness go? Why is it so hard to be thoughtful of the other person's feelings and consider how certain actions will affect them? The drama in your relationship can be easily avoided if you take the time to really understand what your partner is asking for. If it isn't clear, care enough about their concern to ask questions instead of automatically getting offended and defensive. We tell ourselves that the dysfunction we've grown accustomed to is how it's supposed to be, and that is far from the truth. There has to be 100% effort from you, and 100% from them. You should never have to beg for what you believe you deserve. Someone who loves you will work with you before they walk out on you. Your partner should always be worth sticking around for!

CHAPTER 14

Be Realistic

What does it mean to be realistic when it comes to relationships? A lot of the times people get in relationships for self-serving reasons. It's not always to give, or to share love, like it's supposed to be. The person you are with should not cover, or overlook any of your voids. Covering a void is not the same thing as filling it. Most people don't want someone who challenges them to strengthen their weaknesses. They want somebody that helps them forget that those struggles are still present. This is a disservice to growth. If you're trying to hide flaws, cover up mistakes, and down play your insecurities, how can you ask, or even expect someone to keep it real with you? Do you give the honesty you want to receive? Do you provide the support you're looking for? Have you become what they need before you've asked them to be everything you want? Be realistic!

For many, the thought of having to be realistic insists that they should focus on the negatives of whatever is in front them. That is not being realistic; it's being pessimistic. To be realistic is to understand the totality of not just the dating process, but the overall process of a relationship. It's having an awareness that you are not in control of every aspect of your life. You're being realistic when you can honestly say that you don't know what the future holds, but you are living in the moment and going to put forth the effort required to maintain your relationship. You make that decision regardless of what the result may, or may not be.

> **Most people don't want someone who challenges them.**

For many of us, facing reality is such a humbling experience. We've all had to do it whether we wanted to or not. Remember that time you thought,

"This is it! I've found somebody I can genuinely see myself being with long-term." You paid attention to the details of who they were and what they contributed to your life. You listened when they needed someone to talk to. You were supportive when they were going through rough times on their job, or had a death in their family. You were everything they told you they needed, but somehow it still wasn't enough. When you really sit back and think about it, all you can do is shake your head. But that time and period of your life wasn't in vain. At the point where the perfect relationship you thought you had shattered at your feet, you were able to see it all so differently. You were forced to draw back from the situation emotionally and see it for what it was and for what it wasn't.

Being realistic is the ability to accept what you don't always understand. You don't focus on every individual detail. You see the bigger picture of what is going on around you. It's like being the person who planned a pretty picnic and cared less about the weather. You've decided that regardless of rain or shine, you're still going to enjoy all you've set out to do. When you see life this way, nothing can stop you. You are bound to find exactly what you are looking for sooner or later.

CHAPTER 15

Expectations or Exceptions?

It happens to all of us on occasion, and usually while our hearts are still healing. We want the next time to be better than the last time, so we come up with our list of credentials that we hand out to someone before they can qualify as being good enough for us. That man has to have a car, a job with benefits, his own home, and a relationship with God. Before she can meet our family, that woman better have a degree, good paying job, her own place, and our friends have to like her. In our mind, all these things sound like they make up the perfect mate. We come up with this list of expectations for a potential suitor based on the things we say we need in a partner in order for the relationship to work. So in the midst of trying to find somebody to fit the mold of our needs, we run into somebody who instead satisfies the desires of our wants, and we proceed without caution. Even though they are cool, they don't quite measure up to the checklist. So what do we do naturally? We start making exceptions for them.

There is a huge difference between what you want and what you need. Your wants are usually the things you lust after. You *want* a man that's a certain height, skin tone, with perfectly straight teeth, a brand new car, and a job that's paying him at least six-figures. But what you need is a man who is patient, loving, and trustworthy, even though he may come as a completely different package than what you'd expect. You say you *want* a woman who has long hair, hazel eyes, and a body that's fit for a magazine cover. But the woman you need is one of virtue, who is wise with her words, hardworking, supportive and show's she has the qualities needed to bring out the best in you. In any situation, are you able to choose somebody that not only fits what you're looking for, but also satisfies your actual needs? Making exceptions to flaunt something that only looks good on the outside does not make people envious of what you have. All the signs are there, but we quickly lose focus and zip right through the warnings because we think we have to have everything that catches our eye. We don't realize that we're ignoring the very things set in place to guide us.

> *We want the next*
> *time to be better.*

The truth is, making an exception for what you want is far worse than setting an expectation of what you need. Once you set the bar, remove your hands from it unless you're raising it. Every time you set the bar and lower it to make an exception, you give off the impression that you don't care about the things that matter. You don't have to make exceptions to be happy. Sure, there are necessary sacrifices to be made when you're trying to grow with somebody, but that doesn't mean you're required to make exceptions just to say you have somebody. Wants, much like emotions and feelings, are temporary. They can change at any moment. Your needs are what sustain you.

> *... go with your gut.*

Expectations are extremely important to a successful relationship. Think of it this way: when you go to apply for a job, there are levels. The entry-level position requires no experience and a limited resume. The mid-level position expects you to have limited knowledge of the job and have a remote area of expertise. The highest-level position expects you to have enough experience to be trusted to uphold a certain standard of excellence. When it comes to your heart, which level are you advertising and opening for? Your heart should be a high-level position. There are no entry, or mid-level spots to be filled when it comes to your love. The easiest way to ensure this is to go with your gut. Know what you need first, and then set your expectations to balance those needs with a fair inclusion of your wants. The person who is really worth giving a chance to will not want to be the exception. They will want to be the one who exceeds the expectation of what you believe you deserve. When you find that person be sure to hold on to them. They're something special!

CHAPTER 16

Next Time

Nothing about getting hurt is easy to deal with, no matter how many times it happens. People will tell you to move on because they think this will help you to heal faster. But it's not that easy when you've invested so much into one person. You can't just forget about everything and start over immediately, because this person was an important part of your life. You shared conversations about your future plans together and you were building a life with them. When you've given a great deal of your time and emotions to someone, you can't just get over it, but it is possible to get *through* it. It takes time to accept what went wrong, especially when you remember all that was once right. However, there comes a time when you have to be willing to open your eyes to the truth of what the relationship was. You can't run from it forever, or play the victim too long. We weren't born to live that way.

> ... *we don't have to prove anything to anybody.*

For most of us, the hardest part about wanting something real, and long lasting, is trying to convince everyone else that we're not crazy for feeling like we deserve it. People act as if you're supposed to settle just to say you have someone. You start a relationship and everyone is happy for you. Your girls want to know who the new guy is, and they want all the details. Your boys think it's cool that you have found someone you like, but they advise you to take it slow. Your significant other becomes a part of your family and your circle of close friends. You become the couple that others epitomize. You both work hard, you have your own individual goals and dreams, and you even look good together. But that's not enough to keep the relationship going strong. Regardless of what others think, you know the details of your relationship behind closed doors. You take the compliments, laugh to lighten the mood in public, smile and exchange kisses, but you're not as happy as people think you are. So what do you do when what you have turns out to be something you're not sure you want anymore? You start to wonder if this is really the person you can see yourself continuing a relationship with. Before you can make a clear decision, you've got so much advice being given to you that you don't know what to think or do. And this becomes a pattern over and over again with people we care about until we become secure enough in ourselves to realize we don't have to prove anything to anybody.

A common misconception many have is that just because the relationship did not work out, means that something went horribly wrong. Everyone does not lie and cheat. Quite the contrary, some people are totally honest in their relationships. It all boils down to two people deciding what works best for both of them. It is said that opposites attract, and sometimes that is true. But then there are times when you realize that what someone wants for their life is completely opposite from what you want. Maybe you like going to church every Sunday because that's how you were raised, while he's content catching the Sunday morning program on television. He may like to travel and do adventurous things, while you may not be an outdoors person, and prefer being at home on the weekends. It doesn't make either of you right or wrong; it just makes you different. At some point, each person has to be willing to bend on what they decide they can't do versus what they refuse to do. You've learned this before and it is important to emphasize it again: you cannot force someone to do something they have no desire to do. Some things take patience and time. Just because they have not changed yet, does not mean they won't. But don't let that thought have you stagnantly waiting on a change that was never promised because the truth is, some things will never change. It's up to you to determine how much time you're willing to give them to compromise on their differences with you.

> ### *Some things take patience and time.*

When it comes to love, you and your partner both deserve something great. It's not about being too picky or having unrealistic expectations. It's about knowing that you've given what you deserve to receive in return. You now have a firm understanding that your experiences, both good and bad, have earned you the right to have a preference. Stay true to yourself even when nobody gets it. It may feel like, "not again!" but if it's not working for you, it's probably not working for them either. Trust your heart even if it means the relationship has to end, or the two of you agree to be just friends. Don't stop believing in love. Something good will come to you as a result of you being strong enough to free yourself and your partner to be happy. It may feel like it's the end for you, but it's not. It's just a matter of time before you have another chance to find exactly what you're looking for.

For the Men *and* the Women

10 Things
To Keep in Mind
When Starting Over

⚷ For the Men ⚷

1. When you're interested, show it. Don't focus on playing it cool by trying to see what she is going to do first. Keep your intentions clear. Be upfront and honest.

2. Nobody wants to feel like they're stuck in limbo. It's either the friend zone or a committed relationship. Make a decision.

3. Don't be afraid of rejection. Somebody has to be willing to put their feelings out there. Take a chance.

4. Get out of your own way. Pride is the greatest enemy to your happiness. Learn to let things happen naturally.

5. Do little things to show her she's valuable to you. This will remind her of the reasons she chose to be with you.

♥ For the Women ♥

1. Over thinking only complicates things. When your fears have you looking too deep into a situation, it creates unnecessary problems.

2. If you rush it, you might ruin it. If you ignore it, you might lose it. Timing is everything.

3. You can't be afraid to have certain conversations. It's better to communicate than to assume.

4. Different does not mean defective. Get to know him before you reject him.

5. Don't undervalue reassurance. Make sure it's known that the effort being shown by him is acknowledged and appreciated.

10 Ways
To Make the
Relationship Work

⚜ For the Men ⚜

1. A relationship works best when there is an equal balance of giving and receiving. Don't expect her to invest more than you are willing to.

2. There are no real rewards without risk.

3. Don't hesitate to show her how a real man loves a woman. If she's never seen it before, be the example.

4. Be patient enough to make it right, committed enough to make it strong, and honest enough to keep it pure.

5. Don't demand instant perfection. Give the relationship time to develop and grow.

♥ For the Women ♥

1. Don't dwell on what went wrong in your previous relationships. Accept the past for what it is and move on.

2. Set reasonable expectations. Make it clear what you want without making him feel like he is being forced to give it to you.

3. If he says he's willing to do the work, give him a chance to prove himself.

4. Instead of constantly telling him all the reasons he should be with you, consistently show him.

5. Don't compare him to other men in your life. Allow him to be an individual and respect him for who he is.

10 of the Worst Assumptions to Make

⚜ **For the Men** ⚜

1. Don't assume that ignoring the problem will solve it or make it go away.

2. Don't assume that she can read your mind. Be clear, direct, and open to talking. Get accustomed to communicating if you want it to last.

3. Don't assume love will be easy. It's more than passionate feelings and sweet words. You have to always be willing to work at it.

4. Don't assume second chances are guaranteed. The good one's don't go backwards often. Take advantage of what you have or be prepared to miss out.

5. Don't assume that just because you think you want it, that means you automatically deserve to have it. You only deserve what you have worked for.

♥ For the Women ♥

1. Don't assume that fussing and fighting with him will solve the problem. Healthy communication strengthens while bad communication destroys.

2. Don't assume you know more than you do. If you have questions, ask.

3. Don't assume he doesn't care about your feelings. Guard your heart, but remember he has one too.

4. Don't assume that a lasting relationship has to be perfect. Learn to enjoy the good and endure the bad.

5. Don't assume that words can replace effort. Actions always speak louder.

10 Realistic
Relationship Tools

⚑ For the Men ⚑

1. Don't be afraid to show her your emotions. This will build your trust and confidence in her to be there for you.

2. Understand the core values of the relationship. She's looking for someone who can be intimate with her heart— and that stretches far beyond being sexual with her body.

3. There is no master plan to a great relationship. It takes two people who truly *want* to make it work.

4. Compatibility is important. Own who you are and appreciate who she is. Opposites can attract.

5. It is better to try and risk being rejected than to possibly pass up someone great.

♥ **For the Women** ♥

1. Don't make him carry the unnecessary baggage from your past. Let go of anything that has the potential to ruin your relationship.

2. Don't be so invested in learning who he is, that you forget who you are.

3. Trust issues can easily become excuses. A man will only try so many times before he gives up and finds someone else.

4. If you're not committed to the relationship, you shouldn't be in it. Time wasted is unfair to both of you.

5. There's nothing wrong with knowing what you deserve. If you are happy and he's really right for you, he will be happy too.

Additional Book Titles and Audio CD by Rob Hill Sr.
May be purchased on his website:
www.RobHillSr.com

"For Single People Who Still Understand The Value
of Relationships."
ISBN: 978-0-9653696-7-1

"The Audacity Of A Good Heart"
Available in CD and downloadable MP3 formats

Contact Rob Hill Sr.

Email: rob@robhillsr.com

Website: www.RobHillSr.com

Instagram: @robhillsr

Twitter: @RobHillSr

Facebook:www.facebook.com/R0BHILLSR

WITHDRAWN

CPSIA information can be obtained at www.ICGtesting.com
Printed in the USA
LVOW05s2210230214

374893LV00007B/90/P